Winter rain and other poems

Randi Modin

BookLeaf Publishing

Presentation by *BookLeaf Publishing*

Web: www.bookleafpub.com

E-mail: info@bookleafpub.com

ISBN: 9789357211031

First edition 2022

DEDICATION

For my girls,

Always try.

ACKNOWLEDGEMENT

I wouldn't be the person I am if it weren't for the people around me who impacted my life, whether positively or negatively. So shout out to my family (you colorful lot), my friends (you sassy buggers) and my trials (here's looking at you, you bunch of Richards).

PREFACE

I used to enjoy writing poetry so much but now barely write a poem a year. I can't across a writing challenge to write a poem every day...I failed. I wrote but a lot of it stunk. That's ok though, because I was writing. This book is filled with poetry from my past and present, mostly reflective and emotion filled, but here all the same.

... And it was beautiful

The ground was covered in ice,
a perilous sea lay before me.
Almost like lifes indiscrepencies,
lying here and there, all before me.

Sorrow has a small place in my heart,
like a tiny stain that will never go away.
should it spread I would be grateful,
it would make not such a scene.
Just like me, so small,
in this ocean of uncertainty.
Like a beautiful blanket of heart break
ruined by my presence.

The dawn came today and it was beautiful.
I didn't see it, I just knew.
I was blinded by my sheets,
my empty hurt kept me tangled somehow.

As I walked forward I slipped,
not falling in or out.
Wish I could see why I just glided across,
across that plane.
As if I was a crazy dancer,
I moved across on a grace that was not my own.
Silence was my partner,
and it was beautiful.

The scent of smothered blossoms

the scent of orange blossoms drifted through the
air
of a shady cluttered bedroom.
A cascade of cold sunlight drifted through
the blinds of a corner window.
A dreamy kind of state that lulls the senses.
Sacred only to your piece of mind,
and no one elses.
A constant wave of heat thrums from a tiny
silver heater.
And if you sit just right,
the heat and drowsy light, the clutter and the
blossoms,
keep away the cold outside.
Combined, they hint at the happier times.
Summer times when youth kept hurt at bay,
if only for one more season, one more day.

A touch from the floor throws back the present,
The sactuary just a place.
A thought held dear when nothing else is.
Dust shifts through the light,
glittering as if made of gold.
If the sound of life were to take its place,

Show the world outside would you hear?
Sitting on a bed that knows you too well,
here the hair turns grey, the skin begins to fade.
The minds eye begins to dim,
The memory just a feeling of a feeling.
Sacred only to your heart,
and no one elses.
Tragic really to see the attention
captivated by the vast forgetfulness of you.

Just to smell those orange blossoms, just to taste
summers kisses, one more time,
when summer has come and gone.

The art of standing alone

stand alone is a burden,
when wounded and weak,
I sway off kilter...

In this decandent hall of mirrors
Where every wall has my face,
I look to each one
and see a stranger standing in my place.
Where I am weak, she is strong.
Where I am sad, she laughs hard and long.
Each of these faces says the same
When none of them say who I am.

Look, you have fallen and hurt yourself,
I move to help you up when she does not.
A wounded look tells me you don't understand,
that I would hold out my hand, yet,
She turned around and ran.

To stand alone is such a burden,
when tired and cold,
I would just fall...

If she were not so determined to stand...

Winter Rain

Winter rain chills the night,
I, alone, in the dark have walked.
Walked the craggy sidewalk cliffs,
The root snarled forgotten pavement,
Searching for hidden solace.

Hope abandoned me on the evening breeze,
As it crept by slow and slicing.
My heart is tired and heavy with heat,
Keeping my limbs moving among this freeze,
Keeping me from falling into ice.

What is this yearning? This nauseous ache deep
within?
I have felt this rot before, this feeling of
uncertainty that comes to the fore?
It has conquered me before,
This illusion of trust and sparks,
 And sunset rushing through my veins.

Bile, both verbal and not has risen in my throat,
Finally mingling with rain turned to shards on
these empty streets.
Yes, body. Mind. Heart! Empty this out,
Into the stark brutal night!
I will not fall prey again to a lover's plight!

My love is a weed

My love is a weed
It grows in cracks
From root or seed.
I love you as a friend, a lover, as family
No matter who you are,
You are special and will always matter to me.

My love is a weed
Hard to kill from cold or hate
Will not wither in the heat.
Let it fill your cracks and empty places
No matter what you do
My love will flower in forgotten spaces.

My love is a wildflower
Mistaken for noxious weed
But has a healing power.
It grows without help in any dirt
There are no expectations
So just let it heal your hurt.

My love is a wildflower, a herb, a weed
Pick the flowers, the roots, the leaves
It gives freely what you need.

You being you was the seed.

© Randi Modin

Haiku 1

To call it a weed
By judgement of strength through plight
Is human folly

Haiku 2

Spring in the mountains
Sunshine fights with snow and rain
Birds sing anyway

Haiku 3

Neverending growth
Life gives it to you daily
Don't forget to breath

Sunflower

A small daughter
Placed in my arms,
So small, so sweet,
So full of little charms.

She grows like a sunflower
Tall and bright,
So calm, so sweet,
So full of light.

I weep to see
That little girl wilt.
So small, so unsure,
So injured by every slight.

I would keep her in the sun
Away from every storm.
So sweet and bright,
But every flower needs some rain.

Shattered

Shattered heart,
Shattered pieces tossed apart.
They glitter in the dark,
Bite out of sight
And shy from the light.

Pick them up,
Pick them up and hold them close
Each pricking, each drawing blood.
Shiny little sharp hurts
Recalling memories in painful spurts.

Placed together on the wall
They give the reflection of a broken doll.
Tossed and dropped,
She's lost her luster
And her hair falls out.

Maybe there is no fixing this,
This shattered heart.
Let it turn to dust in the dark,
Painful edges dulled with time,
Doll eyes dimmed and filled with spite

Strange how that sounds

Restless feelings seem to consume
the thought of yesterday, tomorrow, and today.
Where there was once a compassion,
I find an empty hole.
Little by little it all changes.
depression, like a sweet slumber,
fills in the empty places.
Calm and quiet I stole into your heart,
and then I ate it whole.
Perhaps it was dream, you say.
Yet when you woke up, I know,
you thought of me first.
Then you thought of death,
an escape from the ache.
Breathing in the stench of broken hearts,
I had to turn to you.
I could almost be sick with the passion.

The rain storm fell down the hill,
becoming a mist that tasted of tears.
The insanity was almost palpable.
and I found the wretch I am,
curled on the ground, sobbing for you.
A becoming of the worst kind of devotion.

Yet it was all a mistake,
when I knew you would not be near.
You, I knew, ran from the fear of me.
Typical of the person you were,
but so strange of the person you now are.
Somehow I felt you should be on a pilgrimage,
to some unknown love that wasn't me,
The me of yesterday. Perhaps not the me of
today.
But possibly the me of tomorrow.
Strange how that sounds,
when the damning soaks through the skin.

With glasses and masquerade masks

A twirl of colors is never ending
in this place i have often seen
behind rose colored glasses
and masquarade masks.
Here we dance to tribute the old.
and the new.
you and your kind. me and mine.
I take a bow to show my sincere respect
and give you thanks.
With grace we change places
and I can see what you really are.
I've decended to a place of make-believe
and hidden laughter.
And the music plays on. I find myself trapped
in the steps.
Never-ending smiles,
hiding the sorrows of yesterday.
And anticipating the joys of tomorrow.

A twirl of colors is never ending
in a place I have often dreampt
behind shattered glasses
and broken masqurade masks.
Here we dance to tribute the truth.

and the lies.
Our kind. and their kind.
I take a bow to end the show
and begin anew.
but with grace we stay the same.

Unfortunate lover

Sad man, bad man, do you need a lover?
I can be your paramore,
help you forget your sorrow.
Love with your body, love me with your words,
and I will love you with my heart.
I will keep you safe in my arms
and help heal your wounds.
Such a sad man, holding out for hope,
you have such a past
and it is just so so sad.
I want to take away your pain.
Bad man, i believe you, you can change.
Hate me with your body, hate with your words,
and I will love you with my heart.

Such an unfortunate lover I am,
To take you in. I will fix your wounds,
build you up and make you whole again.
Such an unfortunate lover I am,
As you heal and leave,
tear me apart and break me down
and leave me full of holes.

Sad man, Bad man,
make me your paramore
I'll break my heart
being your unfortunate lover.

Librarian

Books, books, and more books.
Books on plants, dragons, and romance,
Stories with magic, villains, and defiance.
Recipes to heal... and to poison.
Instructions to build, create, and enjoy some...
party days.
Books for crying,
Books filled with suspense,
Tomes of horror,
Codices of medicinal formulae,
And cheap paperback sci-fi forays.
History, science, nature, and math,
Theory, both philosophical and quantum,
Hide between volumes that inspire hope and
encourage pandemonium.
Books, books, and more books.
A home filled with knowledge, laughter, and
imagination,
That is exactly why I have not a living room but
a library.

Just this once

I ask that you choose me
Not drugs,
Get high on our laughter.
I asked that you choose me
Not drink,
Get drunk off our love.
I asked that you choose me
not suicide,
Escape the pain with our long talks.
I ask that you choose me
and not another,
let us together be enough.
Just this once...
Choose me.

Bindweed

There was a hole in my heart,
where hurts were tossed,
like bodies in the dirt.

I used the broken pieces,
the hurts and memories,
like compost and tried to plant flowers.

I planted seeds of love,
I planted seeds of joy,
I planted seeds of empathy,
And waited for them to grow.

I asked others to water and enjoy;
They watered with abuse,
They watered with drugs and drink,
They watered it with suicide.

There's a pit in my stomach,
where the weeds of my trauma grow like bind
weed in the dirt.

I pull out the roots,
The branching, stabbing hurts,
But I'm still suffocating under it all.

Untitled

"for 4 years I've been dead,
been replaced by a skipping girl
in the hospital Halls of my head."
That's what she told them,
that's what she said.

Damaged parts splayed out
In the eyes of professional strangers,
She kept her cool until she couldn't, Then left
yourself exposed to social pressures.

For years I've been asleep,
Blanketed by the wreckage that I keep,
Replaced by a haphazard me
Digging into the ruins of the garden inside my
head.
That's what I told them,
That's what I said.

Damaged parts tugged out
By court ordered therapy;
I kept my cool until I couldn't,
And I cracked the calm face
I tried to keep in place.

Little girl, lost in the corridors,
I'm waiting here.
I'm racing the clock
And pulling at the weeds.
When you leave the dark
I'll be here
Making a garden for you in my heart.

Little deer

Stars strewn across the night sky,
Sparkle like the laughter in your eyes.
I would like still and hold my breath,
To watch you dancing in the spring breeze.
Hope blossoms with every step you take
You save me from my own destruction and
Hubris.
Cocoa trusses streaming behind
The little deer skipping through the trees.
I sit still and hold you close when I catch and
embrace,
Just to breathe in the dusty sunshine on your
skin.
You bring me back to life;
There's no love felt,
 like the love of a parent for their child.

Joy

Stepping outside into an unknown day,
Filled the smells of growth and decay,
Bird song feels the air with joy.
Sunshine or rainfall,
Snow or wind,
No matter the weather,
I raised my face to the sky
and let the grounding begin.
Sinking my hands into the soil
of a well-turned pot,
Or walking barefoot and grass, gravel, or on
sidewalk,
I can feel the connection I had almost lost.
Bees buzz and land on my shoulder,
Then fly off to pollinate tree and flower.
Deer and turkey trapse through Bush and brush,
And you can still hear the thrum of life,
Even in the hush.

Haiku 4

Early morning rise
Birds and stars mingle at dawn
Quiet calm delight

Like the seasons

I've loved before,
Like a flame,
Consuming everything.
I burned bridges,
And left myself,
Covered in grief burned scars.

I've loved before,
Like a storm tossed sea,
Drowning in all of the emotion.
I drenched obsession
Over us both,
And was left out of breath.

I've loved before,
Like a runaway train,
Leaving wreckage in my wake.
Running over bystanders,
Leaving emotional casualties along the way.

Was it love,
To love this way?
Yes, some would say.
But it is not the way
That I love you.

I love you like the seasons,
Ever changing, yet the same.
Full of growth and laughter,
Full of acceptance and calm,
I weather every storm.

I have loved before,
With destructive force.
I love you now,
With a different love,
Filled with passion and grace.